AF796571

RAW TRUTH

Real Authentic Wisdom

Kirk Alexander & Keith Castille

RAW Truth

Real Authentic Wisdom

Kirk Alexander & Keith Castille

ISBN (Print Edition): 978-1-66788-326-7

ISBN (eBook Edition): 978-1-66788-327-4

© 2022. All rights reserved. No part of this publication may be reproduced, distributed, or transmitted in any form or by any means, including photocopying, recording, or other electronic or mechanical methods, without the prior written permission of the publisher, except in the case of brief quotations embodied in critical reviews and certain other noncommercial uses permitted by copyright law.

DO NOT LOOK FOR THE FINISH LINE JUST COMMIT TO STARTING

Our lives are determined by moments in time. The lives we live, the people we encounter, and the stories we tell create a picture of what we are and who we are. Other people's expectations of us are not always known, unless they have a need or a want for our existence in their lives. The truth is, it is not about them, and it is not even about us. The *them* I refer to are the individuals who do not bring value to our lives. However, we cannot be blind to the fact that our destiny as human beings is to affect the lives of those around us positively. We are to live a life of purpose and search for the why that drives our motivation to an end state that we will be proud of.

We came together to change the narrative. It is not where you are from. Believe it or not, it is not where you are in life either. It is who you are intrinsically, and it can bring out the best of who you are and then the best in others. We are fascinated by positive change and the ability to grow amid adversity. Neither of our lives was easy. Quite frankly, we are glad they were not. We tell our stories from multiple lenses. Whether you are in the boardroom, president of a record label, or an entrepreneur creating your brand, this book is for you. It is about you. It is written so we can learn from each other and commit to better ways of thinking and behaving.

As you read these stories and internalize the meaning of the text, two questions come to mind: How are you living today? Where will life take you tomorrow? Failure to act on the things that you are deficient in does not help to create a better you. To know and not do is not sufficient in this day and age; as a matter of fact, it is a complete disservice to yourself and to those who believe in you or depend on you. This world is hungry for men and women who are ready to be bold and courageous. We are not selling dreams. We offer hope. We hope that what you will become after reading this is far better than the version of you that you are today. We ask that you commit yourself to change lives, organizations, and your community. Be that change our world needs, and, most importantly, do it for the person you stare at in the mirror every day: You. Own it!

Accountability and responsibility start with each and every one of us. Accountability for our own actions is critical for our growth and for not making repeated mistakes or perpetuating generational curses. Responsibility for our own hiccups is crucial to being self-aware, but there are times when we have to fix or remove ourselves from an environment that is broken. Our life lessons help connect what a person values to living out principles that are actionable. It takes a village to raise good followers and great leaders. We are happy you have chosen to be a part of our community. Love y'all for seeking continual growth!

REAL

The R in RAW stands for Real. First, what does *real* actually mean? I am sure we are all familiar with the expression "keeping it real." Depending on where you grew up or the environment you find yourself in at any given time, that term can have a lighter meaning or, for some, can lead to severe consequences such as prison time or death. We all have varying interpretations of what it means to be real. Something we thought long and hard about was the following question: Whom do you have the responsibility to be real to? Do you have to be real to where you are from or rep a particular set? Not in this book!!

First and foremost, you must be 100 percent real to yourself. There is a weight that holds some people down because they feel a responsibility to be real to their city, neighborhood, culture, or childhood friends. It is detrimental to your growth when you're overly concerned with what people think of you and whether or not you're keeping it real for them. It can lead to finding yourself in dangerous environments or situations that you know you don't belong in. We're here to tell you that you should never feel guilty for outgrowing your environment. It is actually what is supposed to happen. If we don't surpass where those who preceded us topped off, then we either weren't given the knowledge by or we refused to heed the advice and lessons of those who came before us. We may not always have someone in our lives to directly pass down lessons to us, but if we observe the lives of others closely, we are able to decipher which paths to take and which to avoid.

Being real is learning, growing, and passing that valuable information to whoever is willing to receive it. If someone who has been part of your life is comfortable where they are and you stay on that level so they feel comfortable, you're not being real to yourself. This is especially true when you know you are capable of achieving so much more. The most real thing you can do is to strive for and reach your goals to become an inspiration for others. Being real is taking the good and bad experiences that shaped who you are and using them to achieve your goals.

As we, men or women with spouses and children, grow our families, our responsibility shifts from ourselves to our family's well being. All decisions you make must be in the best interest of yourself and your family. You are not responsible for the streets or anyone else that would require you to be put in a situation that would be detrimental to you or your family. Being true to yourself and your family is what being real truly is. Holding yourself and others in your circle accountable for being a person of character, integrity, and commitment to reaching goals is the best version of being real we can think of. When you witness someone in your circle moving in a way that is detrimental to them or their family and you have that tough talk about getting them on track, that's real. As you read the stories that have been shared in this book, examine how you may have handled the situations based on who you are. If you find yourself in a situation and you're not sure if being real is the best route, ask yourself this question: Is what I'm doing putting me in the best position to win in every aspect of my life? Keep it real to yourself, your family, and that circle of friends who are people of character who hold each other accountable.

AUTHENTIC

The A in RAW stands for Authentic. Authentic in its most simple form means to be genuine; it is also considered authentic when the origin cannot be disputed. The reason that the A in RAW stands for authentic is that we share our own authentic experiences and those of individuals we've interviewed for the writing of this book. We all have an authentic experience with the interactions of this thing we call life because our backgrounds, DNA, upbringing, culture, race, gender, and so on give us our own individual experience that is uniquely authentic to each of us. There are so many books and videos that tell you how you should act or feel. Influencers supply a steady dose of content for your consumption that shows them consuming or purchasing whatever they are marketing at the moment. It is important that you resist the need to portray yourself as something you are not. It may work in the short term, but it is not sustainable. In order to be successful and maintain a high level of success, you must remain uniquely authentic to who you are.

Understand that we are not telling you to refrain from changing or evolving as a person. All growth requires us to change in some form or another, whether it is physically, emotionally, or mentally. It also doesn't prevent you from being a chameleon and seamlessly adapting to different environments. It doesn't make you fake to be able to speak slang in the neighborhood or use vulgarity among friends on the weekend, then transition to the boardroom as a polished executive on Monday. Your various life experiences and growth grant you the ability to move through drastically different circles. You can be different versions of yourself in different environments, as long as each version is authentic to you. Mimicking someone else's life will only get you so far.

Deliver your story as only you can tell it and provide feedback or speak on topics and issues with authenticity. No matter what industry you're trying to break through in, the key is to be your authentic self. The artist Drake once said in an iHeartRadio interview that the key is to be yourself. He mentioned that in the world of rap, the same things have been said so many times in so many ways and that the only way to stand out is to say things in your own unique way because no one can say them like you. If you think about it, the same can be applied to any field or industry. Don't get it twisted and think simply being authentic is enough to be successful. Your unique authenticity is what will set you apart once you have built a foundation of skills, tools, and the knowledge required to excel in your particular area of expertise. Keep grinding and putting in the work to become the most authentic version of the person you are meant to be.

WISDOM

The W in RAW stands for Wisdom. When thinking about wisdom, one may think of the old heads that begin to tell us war stories about what they did and the creative adventure behind those things. We look at wisdom in a multitude of ways. Wisdom is taking what was learned, finding value in the lessons imposed, and then sharing it with someone. They can either learn from it, apply it, or share it with their circle of influence. Throughout our years, wisdom from the elders has guided us to some great decision-making and weighing the pros and cons of choices we can potentially make.

Organizational wisdom is guided through climate and culture. One may have all the wisdom in the world but choose not to share based on their personal values or their willingness to be transparent and team-oriented. There are also some organizational cultures that groom the thought-provoking process that brings in diverse perspectives to solve problems. Wisdom is critical to connecting pathways to the past and moving forward with ideal solutions. With our upbringing, wisdom has been broken down into this acronym that just makes sense:

W— **W**illing to share

I— The **I**ntegrity of the information is intact. What is known to be true through various checking sources?

S— **S**elfless when **S**haring. It is not about you. The information is meant to add value.

D— **D**uty to protect what you say coming out of your mouth, and you will stand by it.

O— **O**pportunity for another person to learn and grow. It helps to create generational knowledge.

M— **M**alleable can stand the test of time and be shaped or articulated to connect to any generation or environment one is in.

Wisdom is about pouring into others the knowledge you have gained or have access to that will shape the way another person thinks to positively make a difference in their lives. Without wisdom, we are a generation lost. Our society will perish because there is no golden knowledge to active thought that encapsulates vision. Wisdom is emotional intelligence. It is the foundation of deliberate thinking that weighs reactions and the effects of one's action.

Personal wisdom is placing oneself in the arena with repetitions both leading and following at different levels. It is the attitude that one cannot just sit around and expect that things are going to fall in your lap. Wisdom is a personal choice to place oneself in uncomfortable situations where growth, failure, and vulnerability shape future narratives. The art of wisdom is connecting what a person believes to what they are willing to die for. Wisdom is trust disguised as a charcuterie board that pulls at your senses. Allow it to flow through your mind, absorb its value, and apply it to your life where it makes sense.

TABLE OF CONTENTS

#RAW

Real Authentic Wisdom

The inspiration for RAW can be attributed to a multitude of shared experiences, perspectives, and situations in our lives. While growing up in Lafayette, Louisiana, we have experienced plenty of RAW or truths that helped to shape our lives. It is one of those places where people speak without a filter and tell you exactly what is on their minds. Our experiences, from the neighborhood to the military and working in civilian life, have all played a part in developing these raw truths. They have shaped our perceptions and our ability to think critically and be reflective thinkers. When we first developed the concept for this book and decided to move forward, the intent was to tackle or address some areas that were not typically discussed. We wanted to give people some *Real Authentic Wisdom* based on situations that occur across all facets of a person's experience, like business, life, military, and so on. It also provides information to contribute to the self-development of yourself and others. We aim to present the RAW and provide a real-life scenario, tip, and a quote so that you can reflect on it and incorporate it into your personal and professional lives.

Tip

Always find a way to use your experiences and circumstances to contribute to future success.

Quote

"By three methods we may learn wisdom: First, by reflection, which is noblest; second, by imitation, which is easiest; and third by experience, which is the bitterest."— "Confucius, Chinese philosopher and politician of the Spring and Autumn period."

How to Navigate This Book

1. Storyline
2. Connection to Life
3. Tip to Consider
4. Quote to Ponder
5. Internalize, Think, Act, Do—Share

Keith's Personal Perspective

RAW is personal to me. Let's go!!!!! When Kirk and I decided to write this book, it excited me to share some space with my best friend of thirty years. We grew up near each other and attended the same schools growing up. Our lives were different in a few ways, but we had one thing in common: We always strived for greatness. The roads here are not easy. We scraped our knees many times while sacrificing our minds, bodies, and spirits. We were in a zero-sum game. We could either let the streets devour us and become a statistic or grind until the wheels fall off.

Throughout my life, I have been spit on, counted out, disfavored, and pushed to the side to rot. Mentors grabbed hold of me and demanded I change the narrative that I was creating in my life. That scared me, because I did not feel that I was the problem. The truth was, when looking in the mirror you are always the problem because you get to choose what version of yourself you want to be. RAW helps you choose who you need to be, not who you want to be, based on others' perceptions.

When I was thirteen, I started going to the Boys and Girls Club. This was a cool place to hang out in the neighborhood. It shielded me from drugs and crime. I was exposed to new things and new opportunities. Without it, I feel that my chances of being where I am in life today would not be the same. More than twenty-eight years since my last official encounter with the Club, the things I learned still help guide me today. Did I fumble? Did I fall? The answer is yes. I continue to fail. Fortunately, I created a routine that led to a mindset shift focused on my faith, family, and nation.

I am on a mission. This mission is to change lives and build a world that is loving, compassionate, empathetic, and committed to understanding each other on a human level. My words are not meant to tear anyone down. My goal is to build leaders and followers who will dedicate their lives to the service of others. The words and stories that I provided while penning in this book will never portray me as a victim. I am courageous and victorious. My heart and head are in the game. Now it is time to share with the world.

Kirk's Personal Perspective

Circumstances from growing up in Lafayette, Louisiana, all the way to living in Ramstein, Germany, as a military spouse have all shaped my perspective on life. I have had the opportunity to meet and experience many people along the way who have affected me in some form or another. My goal is to be the type of person who always makes a positive impact on the people I have the opportunity to interact with. I want to share a little bit about some of the people who have affected me and shaped me into the person I am today.

At the tender age of twelve, I lost my father, who passed away while undergoing surgery. I was left with only my mother, Verna Alexander, as a parent. I quickly realized what the strength of a strong woman looked like. She made sure I had everything I needed and most of what I wanted. In those days, we were truly raised by a village, and I was supported by many in that village who I would like to quickly highlight.

Mr. Jessie Thomas is the father of my childhood best friend Floyd "Meaux" Thomas, who I've known all my life. Jessie was the first man to really open my mind and encourage me to see a life beyond the city we lived in. I was inspired by the stories he shared about his time in the Air Force and his travel experiences. He coached us in basketball, but more importantly, he coached us to be men. He and his wife, Jackie, were also the first frame of reference I had of a strong, loving marriage between two people who were working hard to build a life for each other and their family.

Mr. John "Shortstop" and Rose Chevis were the parents of my best friend and neighbor John "Boo" Chevis. Mr. John was my example of a man who put in a tremendous amount of work for his family and was also a man of very few words. I observed that when he did speak, everyone stopped and listened. Not because of fear, but because he didn't waste his words so people valued them when they were spoken. His actions showed his phenomenal work ethic. The house he built for his family was a mansion in my eyes and to many others in the neighborhood. I spent many nights there and was inspired to own a mansion of my own for my family one day. Aunt Rose, as I called her, was like a second mother looking out for me. I knew if my mom was hard at work providing for me, there was always a hot meal just across the street waiting for me. She also wasn't shy about calling me out if I got out of line, and would inform my mother about it, who didn't play about not conducting yourself in a positive and respectful manner.

I realize that not everyone has a support system or a village to help raise them. Many are in environments that are not conducive to growth and are filled with landmines that can derail you at a moment's notice. I would like to share that in my village I also observed many people whose behaviors were not positive. Being able to observe from others what not to do can be just as valuable. Learning from the negative behaviors and missteps of those around you is critical to breaking generational curses and moving beyond the negative or hopeless circumstances. Because my eyes are always open to learning, I want to share an experience of mine.

Recently, I decided that I would undergo Lasik surgery to correct my vision so I could stop wearing glasses. At the pre-op appointment, I was given a packet to read and initial about the procedure. It went over the possible risks involved and expectations for after the surgery. What stood out to me the most were the explanation of how the procedure would be performed and the aftercare requirements. The procedure starts by making an incision into the cornea of the eye to create a flap. Then the laser goes in, section by section making the necessary corrections. As a coach, speaker, and trainer, I'm always evaluating situations from that perspective to see if they can be used as teaching moments.

The process of correcting my vision seemed to have a direct parallel with the often-painful experiences we go through to heal ourselves or make improvements in our lives. Similar to Lasik surgery, in order for a correction or improvement to take place in our lives there first has to be an incision made in order to peel back the layers and examine what needs to be corrected or healed. Once we identify what needs to be corrected, we develop a plan of action to achieve the desired results. We must go section by section when making the corrections to ensure the desired results are achieved. If we fix one area and neglect others, we open ourselves up to complications.

The next thing that stood out to me was the extreme level of aftercare that was required to maintain the corrections and not cause damage to the repaired areas. It stated that I was to keep water and dust out of my eyes for three to four months. I thought to myself, *How in the hell am I supposed to do that?* It is a difficult, but necessary, step in the aftercare process. There were other steps, such as placing eye drops three times a day to moisturize the eyes, along with follow-up appointments. All of these steps were working together to obtain the goal of corrected vision. When you work on yourself to make significant growth or heal from trauma, it will also require some aftercare steps and follow-up.

Knowing that you may have to remove someone stressful from your life or not put yourself in situations where you're forced to resist temptation is daunting. As resilient humans, we often find ways to heal ourselves, whether that is through our own discoveries or receiving the guidance of a professional. Where we sometimes fail is with aftercare. We can't allow ourselves to be in situations that may trigger old traumas or hang out in circles with the same individuals responsible for the traumas. How diligent you are in the aftercare process will be the determining factor in sustaining what you've achieved. If you put in the work to heal, change, or improve yourself, complete the process by ensuring you take the appropriate aftercare steps for long-term success.

TIME DOES NOT STOP

Although time waits for no one, there are things we can do to maximize it. Are you using your time effectively, or does time fly past you? Be conscious and present of what occupies your time and decide on whether what you are doing is worth your time and effort.

Scenario

Bill is thirty-six years old. For the last ten years, Bill has wanted to go on a cruise. Unfortunately, he has never made time for the things he loved. He spent four years in Germany and never visited another European country. Last week Bill found out that his close friend Sam was diagnosed with a rare form of cancer and had six months to live. Sam wants Bill to accompany him on an adventure, knocking out things on his bucket list. Bill's perspective on life is rapidly changing because …

Perspective

I am sure you have heard the saying "time waits for no one." That is a statement that could not be truer in both life and business. Time is exceptionally fair and consistent in its treatment of us all. Regardless of what your plan is, time will continue moving along. Don't become stagnant, waiting for the right or perfect time to do something. If it is what you truly desire, then now is always the right time to commit and go for it. What is the cost you pay if you don't, or never get a chance to do that one thing you wanted?

Although time doesn't stop, you can change your perception of it so it seems to be slowing down. If you move at the same pace as time, it will appear to slow down. If you continue the same routine and do not allow your brain to experience anything new, then time moves quickly. Tricks to slow down the perception of time could be indulging in new experiences, taking in new information, driving a different, unfamiliar route to work, or trying a new restaurant. Take advantage of the time you have by finding new ways to improve and enrich yourself. Take in everything around you and appreciate it. That may require putting your phone down. It may also require you to spend less time or stay away from people who tend to waste your time. If you had a specified amount of time left on this earth, how would you live it? What would you do? Since no person controls time, what will you do with what you have today?

Tip

Break the habit of simply moving through life and enjoy living your best life.

Quote

"Doing the same routine every day barely registers in the brain. You don't notice it. You don't remember doing it. Thus, entire days are lost."— "Mark Sisson, American fitness author and food blogger."

POINT SHAVING

Your team is up by one point with less than two minutes in the game. Two of your teammates are not giving their all. They lack hustle, drive, and commitment to the team. There seems to be an unequal balance of players on the team. One of your teammates accidentally scores a point for the other team.

Scenario

The game is on the line, and you are one stop from securing the win. However, a teammate of yours is more concerned with his individual numbers. He is one rebound away from a triple-double and wants to impress the scouts in attendance. You tapped the floor with both hands and tightened your defense, forcing your opponent into an unbalanced shot that clanged off the side of the rim. Despite a teammate already being in position, your selfish teammate goes after the rebound anyway and inadvertently tips it into your opponent's basket as the buzzer sounds. In unison, everyone in your home stadium is standing, mouth wide open with hands on their heads in disbelief about what just happened …

Perspective

Playing sports in high school afforded me an opportunity to learn life lessons. My coach would always inject some power quotes as he attempted to take a rowdy group of men through a full season of growing pains. He would often ask players on the team if they were playing for our team or the other. He would also ask if we were committed to the team and wanted to win. Based on his assessment of the situation, he was 100 percent correct. Some of us did not want to win. We did not have the fortitude or the ability to push through adversity. A few players quit and others were unable to give themselves fully, so they just went through the motions. They were cancers on the team. Turn in your jersey!

Tip

Know and understand your position on the team. Develop trust amongst your teammates and demand accountability to each other and for each other. Look at areas of your life where you did not give it all you had, you simply gave just enough to get by. Life is not about taking the easy route, and all routes are not easy.

Quote

"We learned about honesty and integrity—that the truth matters ... that you don't take shortcuts or play by your own set of rules ... and success does not count unless you earn it fair and square"— "Michelle Obama, former First Lady of the United States of America."

TURN SHIPS

It will take time. Do not rush progress. Build trust and give autonomy. Accept risk.

Scenario

Sarah has been named the new CEO of the firm. During her first thirty days on the job, she noticed that there was a lack of leadership in three of the four departments. After two months of reviewing assessments and providing responses on culture issues, she makes a recommendation to release two of the department heads. Everyone is concerned because the department heads have been the continuity through multiple change initiatives. However, there has been very little return on investment from 95 percent of the projects currently in the works. Three months after the release of the department heads, progress is trending upward, but it is very slow …

Perspective

The first thirty days are important. You walk into a new organization and notice that things are not what they seem. You called ahead, and all you received was great news about the new team. After a few hours, you realize that the people, resources, and leadership in place do not have a clue. Do not be quick to judge. Steve Jobs once said, "Deciding what not to do is as important as deciding what to do." Listen, learn, and take notes.

Your expertise in prior situations will be valuable. Please be aware that you will not have all the answers. If you have ever taken a cruise, you will realize that the captain turning the ship around is steadily focused on what is ahead and what is to the side of the ship. In other vessels you have ridden in or on, it may take only a second or two to turn around. Your ship (unit/organization) will take time to move from its current state to its future state. Be invested and patient. Building cohesive teams is your number-one goal to get after low performance indicators that are weighing your organization down.

Tip

Discovery interviews are important to uncover the good and the bad. Randomly choose individuals spanning various demographics in the organization. Take notes and look for common themes. Organizing your thoughts and notes is crucial to ensuring that nothing is lost in translation. Remain focused. It is about the long game.

Quote

"Alone we can do so little; together we can do so much."— "*Helen Keller, American author and Presidential Medal of Freedom recipient.*"

YOU CAN'T MANAGE TIME

Stop wasting time trying to manage time. Instead, focus on prioritizing the things that really matter and utilize your time there. Learning to become more results-focused may relieve the stress of trying to manage time.

Scenario

This reminds me of a human resources administrator we interviewed while examining an organization's productivity. Her name was Marie, and she was working until 7 p.m. every day. She was struggling with work-life balance and felt like she didn't have enough time or wasn't managing her time well ...

Perspective

So often, we hear people say that they are great at managing time. What does it really mean when a person says they are a great time manager? I often ask them, "What happens to the time when you stop managing it?" How is time different when you manage it versus when you don't manage time? I believe what most people are trying to imply is that they are great at task management and prioritizing. They understand what needs to get done based on the time they have. Since you can't manage the time, you should focus on managing other things in your control that can allow you to be more effective. Prioritizing essential tasks is more effective than trying to manage time.

Another area we often do not think about or overlook is managing our energy. Try examining what tasks you have to complete and how much energy they consume. Based on your skillset, strengths, and weaknesses, some tasks will drain you while others will energize you. Understanding how your energy is affected can allow you to plan your schedule to maximize task completion. Managing your energy level with people is just as important as with tasks. We often feel like we need to spend a certain amount of time with people, but the energy does not match. For example, if you spend an hour with someone while you're also on your phone or preoccupied, it probably won't satisfy their needs. You can be more effective by giving max energy for a shorter period of time. To be most effective, focus on prioritizing and managing your energy and stop managing time.

Tip

Stop multitasking, focus on what needs to be done, and move to the next item on the list.

Quote

"The shorter way to do many things is to only do one thing at a time."—"Wolfgang Amadeus Mozart, was a prolific and influential composer of the Classic period."

WHAT VALUE ARE YOU LEAVING / TAKING?

Leave it better than you found it. Hell with that! Break it and return it in pieces!

Scenario

While having dinner one night, we had the most phenomenal waiter you could ask for. I asked him how he was so enthusiastic about doing what he does when so many in customer service are disgruntled. He replied that he saw his job as a future investor in his dream …

Perspective

Feedback is important. Especially initial feedback, where a leader or supervisor expresses their rules and expectations. A lot of information is provided. As a person leaves this session, they are reminded to leave it better. Some real talk here: Your time is finite in an organization. Even if you are in a position that allows you to remain stable for a longer amount of time, you may be moved to another area. The roles could change. Corporate does a sell-off, and now your position has either merged or transformed. The point is to make time count for the time you have. Find the required change and bring value to advocating for a solution to that problem. One must also consider what are you taking away each and every day? What fills your cup? What empties it? Value goes both ways, just as growth and opportunities do. Are you thinking about how your current organization invests in your development? Is your growth part of their plan to keep you motivated in providing innovative ideas?

Tip

What knowledge are you leaving behind? Who did you take along to learn how you have done it? Are you serving in a point-of-failure position? Fix that construct. Put some thought into this: What if tomorrow you can't show up at work? No turnover, yet nothing was left to help the incoming hire. What skills or competencies did you focus on during your tenure there? What person do you work with who you can share this knowledge with?

Quote

"You don't get paid for the hour. You get paid for the value you bring to the hour."— "Jim Rohn, was an American entrepreneur, author, and motivational speaker."

BACK TO BASICS? NO

This is not your typical back-to-basics discussion. We are always told to go back to basics when things such as culture, planning, and so on go terribly. That is the wrong answer. Go back to common sense.

Scenario

James is a team member on a large project with multiple stakeholders. His team made a critical error on a report they had been working on for weeks. The product they sent forward caused the entire team to lose two weeks on the project. James became frantic and wanted to do all he could to ensure no more mistakes were made. As he reviewed the mistakes, he noticed that his team was overanalyzing everything. One of the stakeholders provided feedback and stated that he and the team needed to get back to the basics of the project and keep it simple. This was not the approach he wanted to hear from a strategic leader. The team should …

Perspective

The basics are what got you there. The foundation is what keeps you grounded. Clear vision and mission are steering the path. In 2018, I worked alongside a very reputable individual of high character and competence. During this project, she continued to drop the ball on some items that needed her skill sets. We continued to provide support and filled in where needed. Unfortunately, none of us could answer the call due to our lack of knowledge in this arena. Senior leaders came down to our location and heard the problems we were facing. My first words of advice were, "Go back to basics." The problem we were trying to fix failed until a mid-level executive decided to help coach our team through this problem set. Within fifteen minutes of listening to the problem, she made us aware of how our team project integrated into the overall plan. We had missed some strategic steps to integrate our project into the overall design. The coaching was not back to basics, but required critical thinking, strategic planning, and problem-solving skills. This was the traction we needed to push through. The problem was fixed within seventy-two hours.

Tip

Back to basics gets you back to a place with a starting point. Sometimes that is good, but what you want to instill into your work ethic is an innovative mindset. Take a current problem you are trying to fix. Draft a narrative where you can get an outside opinion on the matter. This person does not need working knowledge of what the team is working on, just the skill sets that allow them to work through some problem-solving methodologies. Provide the narrative. Listen to the feedback. Get a second opinion using the same method. Now go to a subject matter expert and articulate the findings. Listen!

Quote

"We can not solve our problems with the same level of thinking that created them."— "Albert Einstein, Theoretical physicist."

SHEEP DOG

A sheepdog does a great job controlling a flock. It knows when to intervene and draw attention to the sheep. Every move is timed and choreographed. But when equating it to humans, one has to see there are benefits and negatives. Know when to move.

Scenario

Floyd is a lead engineer on a government contract. He has been working with a large city to break ground on a multi-billion dollar project. Each time his team gets approval from the city and has permits in hand, a local agency representing a group opposing the project submits a complaint and stalls work. The sides have yet to meet in person to discuss an agreement. There are assumptions that prior personal grudges not related to the project are causing friction. There seems to be no end in sight. Floyd decides …

Perspective

While working with a client, we discussed some things that were bothering him professionally and personally. It seemed that what was causing issues at work was making its way to his home life. On the flip side, what was causing issues at home was being brought to work. He described a situation with his pending divorce that weighed on him heavily. He stated that his ex was a sheepdog. Every response by the opposing team was calculated and timed. They were going to wait him out. It was costly to continue fighting.

There are a myriad of angles from which to analyze this real-world scenario. However, stubbornness seems to be the common theme of both parties. No one was willing to give a little to gain a lot. What is the cost of being stubborn and failing to hear someone else's side? John Maxwell and various other authors are known for saying that "Hurt people, hurt people." Moreover, stubbornness never woke the dead. Learn when to let go and lean on one's strength to move forward.

Tip

Know what gets you stuck and keeps you stuck. Get unstuck. Are you emotional about the situation or passionate about it? Write down a list of things that you are holding on to. Rank order them from most important to least. Discover why it is keeping hold of you. Determine how to let go. Seek assistance where the core theme lies.

Quote

"Some of us think holding on makes us strong, but sometimes it is letting go."— "Hermann Hesse, German-Swiss poet, novelist, and painter."

MANAGE YOUR TALENT

An excellent first step to managing your talent is to first identify what your talents are. This may require you to take an assessment or conduct a self-exploration to identify your talents and strengths.

Scenario

Sarah is up for promotion to the coveted VP position. She has made it past two rounds of interviews. The competition is strong. Sarah is competing against other top managers in the firm, including Donna. Donna has made a name for herself by assembling diverse teams around the nation to solve problems that plagued the company for years. As Sarah prepares for the third and final interview, she has an epiphany that she has not been afforded the opportunity to lead large projects at the regional level. She feels that this may be a deciding factor for the position. Sarah calls her executive coach to discuss ...

Perspective

Managing your talent is critical for your career advancement or running a successful business. What talents are you bringing to the table personally, and what talents do you surround yourself with? Unless you're a sole proprietorship, you should be considering whether the talents of the team around you compliment one another. You have to be in charge of your professional development. Don't be that person who only receives training when they are told to report for professional development. When you do have the opportunity to attend professional development, show up with the intention of improving yourself.

Managing your talent often requires making an investment in yourself. Oftentimes we have to go outside of our organization to receive specialized training. That usually requires you to pay for the full cost of the training necessary to increase your talent level. I have spoken with people who need a single specific training or certification to be able to advance in their organizations. When I ask them why they have not obtained it yet, the answer is, "My company/organization does not pay for that training." It comes down to cost versus value, and if you have the will to get it done. Usually, the value is there, but they are not willing to bet on themselves and accept the cost of improving their talent. You have to take ownership and be the primary manager of your talent.

Tip

You have to want to improve yourself more than anyone else wants you to improve. Take a strengths-finder assessment. Determine what gaps need to be filled. Write down the actions you're willing to take to achieve your level of success. Ensure they are S.M.A.R.T. Revisit them frequently.

Quote

"Be led by your talent, not by your self-loathing; those other things you just have to manage."—"Russell Brand, English comedian and actor."

ALL SIZZLE, NO STEAK

Lights, Camera, Action!

Scenario

Jay was part of a sports team that was preparing for a new season. The coaches went out and recruited top-level talent from around the country. After seeing the talent level that was assembled, expectations for the team were set pretty high. Winning it all was going to be their only option for success. There was no consideration about how these players would gel on and off the field. Although they all had the goal of winning, there were no shared values among the teammates. Jay realized that if everyone didn't put the team goals ahead of their own, it would be a long season. During the season opener, Jay could feel the buzz and excitement moving through the stadium as he stared into the crowd ...

Perspective

The company you keep is the company that seeks you! That can go a variety of ways. I had a wonderful opportunity to provide executive coaching to a professional sports team. This team, on paper, looked good. They had all the key ingredients to have a successful season. At the start of the season, practices were going well. There was a lot of teamwork and sportsmanship. There were high expectations from the fans and front office. The team ended the season 0-14. The players never gelled. No bonds were created. A few friendships were formed, but, for many reasons, ended with major conflict.

We do not always get to choose our teammates. What we do get to choose is our reaction, emotion, and commitment to the team. This team failed to have success due to the off-the-court battles and individual players' inability to see the errors of their ways. The coaches were the center of ridicule. There was an attempt to blame things outside of their control. One could argue that the blame goes to that person's effort, grit, and mindset. Being part of a team comes with major responsibilities. It takes concerted effort and a team mentality. A circle of trust must be formed. The team is only as strong as the weakest link. Someone has to step up and infuse the values and principles that nurture the team to greater possibilities and growth. Every member of the team matters.

Tip

What are your strengths and weaknesses? What are the strengths and weaknesses of the individuals in your circle? Do you complement each other, or is there friction? What value does each person add, both personally and professionally? Transformational friendships, whether personal or professional, lead to growth and commitment to the team and the efforts made.

Quote

"This year, we won't keep company with anger, bitterness, and envy. Our inner circle will include hope, faith, and joy."— "Andrena Sawyer, best selling author, business consultant, and entrepreneur."

I AM HUNGRY

Do not show up to the table expecting to eat if you have not prepared yourself to be fed. Your momma told you not to show up to someone's house empty-handed. Well, the same goes for showing up to the business table empty-handed and expecting to eat.

Scenario

Chris was heading out to lunch to meet up with two of his best friends from childhood, Mike and Chad. When Chris arrived at the restaurant, his friends were in the middle of discussing the sale of a house they were flipping. When Chris heard the projected profit of $70,000, he asked how he could get in on the deal. Chad explained that they had everything covered on this deal, and Chris would not be involved. Chad broke down how he searched and found the deal, how Mike had the financing covered and also found a contractor to perform the work. Chris was livid and felt betrayed. Chris got up from the table and told Chad and Mike ...

Perspective

So many people are hungry to level up in their careers or life, but either forget to meal-prep or are too lazy to prepare in advance. Do not keep telling people that you're hungry and asking for an opportunity to eat if you're not preparing for the meal. Too often, we see individuals asking for opportunities, but they are not willing to do the front-end work necessary to achieve success.

All of their focus is on the end result rather than the intense process required to achieve it. Stop looking for a shortcut to the end and focus on learning every step of the journey to get there. There's a triangle of success made up of the following elements: Knowledge/Experience, Money/Resources, and Opportunity. When you're trying to have a seat at the table, you need to possess one of the three elements. If you do not have the money or experience, then go find the opportunity.

Sometimes we are offered the blueprint to level up in our careers or lives, and all we can focus on are the cost, time, and work required. We may avoid an opportunity because it will take two to four years of reeducation or training to reach it, stating that we will be whatever age by the end of it. You will reach that age regardless of whether you go for it, so why not reach that age with upgraded education or talent to achieve greater success? Anytime you're offered a blueprint to success, access to information, or training, take the leap, especially when it boils down to betting on yourself. You must be willing to bet on yourself and not depend on someone else to place a bet on you. I usually think of the proverb, "Prepare your work outside and get it ready for yourself in the field, and afterward build your house and establish a home." Do not just keep saying, "I'm hungry;" learn to prepare yourself to eat the way you deserve.

Tip

Your input should match your output, meaning you have to own it. Look at the projects you lead or are a team member of. Take note of the triangle of success. What part of the formula do you represent that completes the equation?

Quote

"What's the key to success? The key is, there is no key. Be humble, be hungry, and the hardest worker in any room."— "Dwayne Johnson, American actor and former professional wrestler."

ASSIGNED VALUE

It is time to take back your worth and determine your own self-worth. Only stay in places where you are appreciated rather than where you are tolerated.

Scenario

Windell went in for his yearly employee evaluation at a structural design company and was offered a raise of $1.50 per hour. He accepted the increase from his superior and returned to work. During his smoke break, he asked a coworker Leonard how his evaluation went. Leonard said he rejected the $1.50 per hour raise and asked for $4.50, and they settled on an increase of $3.50 per hour. Windell was furious, because he had been at the company much longer. Leonard asked why he was upset if he accepted the $1.50 raise with no arguments. Windell's only response was that …

Perspective

Only remain in a place where you are valued. This topic jogged my memory about a great story related to assigned value. A father said to his beloved daughter, "Since you graduated with honors, I am giving you a car I acquired a long time ago. It is a really old car, but it has some life left. But before I give it to you, take it to the used car lot downtown and tell them I want to sell it and see how much they offer you." She went to the used car lot, returned to her father, and said, "The dealer offered me $1,000 since it's so worn out." The father then said, "Now take it to the pawnshop." The daughter went to the pawnshop, returned, and told her father, "The pawnshop offered $100 to take it off our hands." Her father instructed her to go to a car club and show them the car. The daughter showed the car to the club members, and she returned and told her father, "Some members of the club offered $100,000 for the car since it's a Nissan Skyline R34, and sought after by many collectors." The father said to his daughter, "The right place will value you the right way." If you are not valued, do not get angry or discouraged. It simply means that you are in the wrong place. The ones who know your value are the ones who will appreciate you. Never stay in a place where no one sees or appreciates your value.

You have to know your worth and put yourself in an environment where you are valued and appreciated. Often when you shed your old self, those around you continue to hold on to that previous version and refuse to acknowledge your change. Sometimes your value will be recognized by displaying newly acquired skills, but you still may not receive the compensation you feel you deserve. It may require shedding the current environment for an entirely new one that will properly recognize your value and what you bring to the table. Most employers want to get a good deal for their money. Do not allow your value to be diminished or discounted only for others to gain.

Tip

Never remain in an environment that does not appreciate the value you bring. You have to bet on yourself. Ensure your voice is heard when decisions are being made that affect you.

Quote

"Only you can make the decision for what you believe your worth is and that will determine how you allow people to treat you."— "Germany Kent, American print and broadcast journalist, television personality, former beauty queen, actress, businesswoman, and producer."

MANATEE

It is okay to be underestimated! Do not concern yourself with trying to look the smartest or wealthiest. Make sure you have what it takes to get the job done and deliver results.

Scenario

Tracy is known as a very reliable teammate. She is the first to enter the building and the last person to leave. She ensures that the team is prepared for all major projects by structuring work tasks and keeping stellar records of performance markers. Tracy is excited about two new projects the company is taking on with a new client. After receiving multiple recommendations from supervisors, she decided to apply for the lead position. As she finalized the last part of the application, she received an email stating that the position had a tentative offer and that no more applications would be accepted. Tracy was hurt that the rules were not followed in the hiring process and she did not get a chance to be considered. Two days later, she found out that Carl had received the position. Carl is not the best candidate. However, he ensures he gets massive amounts of face time and bulldozes others to be the lead presenter. He is not a team kind of person. Carl focuses on pushing his own agenda. Tracy decides to …

Perspective

While managing an office or a business, we often overlook the individuals who are putting in the real work and making a difference. This may be due to perceptions and biases clouding our vision about who the key employees really are. If you are a hard worker, then you tend to look for hard workers that look like you. It reminds me of the differences between a dolphin and a manatee. Both of these mammals are unique and play a vital role in the ecosystem of the ocean. However, they are perceived very differently by most people.

The dolphin is perceived as very swift with its smooth, shiny gray skin and because it communicates with a beautiful sound. In contrast, the manatee is perceived as slow, overweight, and not that appealing to the eye. Most people do not realize that manatees can swim up to twenty miles per hour and, despite having a tiny brain for their size, can be trained to do tricks or tasks similar to a dolphin. The difference is that the manatee is more challenging to train because it is not motivated by fish. They are similar to those employees who are not highly motivated by money. They are capable of contributing just as much as those who appear to be moving fast and looking good. Look beneath the surface, and take note of who is really contributing and living the vision of the organization. Please don't think this analogy is all about looks. It has more to do with investigating who are the real contributors and what their motivations are. You probably have some manatees making major contributions and going unrecognized. Don't risk losing them by focusing too much attention on the perceived stars.

Tip

Become more aware of what your people are doing and which ones are the most valuable players/contributors. Reward those who consistently meet and exceed standards, and hold those accountable who do not.

Quote

"Never confuse movement with action."— "Ernest Hemingway, American novelist, short-story writer, and journalist."

CUTTING WEIGHT

A snake sheds its skin when it has outgrown it.
Don't regret having to let go of people around you
who aren't willing to grow to a new level.

Scenario

Meaux went back home to visit for the first time after enlisting in the military. He had learned new skills and experienced different people and places. His outlook on life had been greatly expanded. While playing dominoes with his friends from the neighborhood, he shared his new experiences. He was not expecting the reaction he received. They told him that he had changed and thought he was better than everyone else. Meaux responded by saying he did not think he was better than them, but that …

Perspective

In order to obtain the next level of success, we must first shed layers. Shedding layers is a complete and voluntary letting go of behaviors or environments that prevent you from leveling up. This can be an extremely difficult, but necessary, process. There are two important aspects to the process of shedding in order to level up. First, we examine ourselves to see if there are any bad habits, destructive activities, or negative pathways of thinking that need to be shed. Next, we take a look at our environment, which may include but is certainly not limited to the following: friends, family, partner/spouse, job, church, or even the city in which you live. When I speak of shedding church, I do not mean your faith; you may simply need a different place or method of practicing your faith. Although difficult, I have found that people have an easier time making personal sheds versus environmental sheds.

Personal sheds require much self-reflection to determine what needs to be changed about oneself. It may also require healing or forgiving, which can be daunting, and, depending on the trauma, it may take speaking with a professional. Later in the book, we discuss routines and how they can keep you down or allow you to level up. Examining your daily and weekly routines is an excellent starting place for personal shedding.

Environmental sheds are the most difficult because the loss feels far greater. Especially when you are at a stable or successful level in your life or career but want to level up, it is easy to shed a shitty job or leave a city where you have nothing established. When you have a life that most people strive for and you have to shed it in order to reach your full potential, that is when considerable courage and dedication are needed. If you are the only person in your circle growing, you may have to shed your entire circle. Ray Lewis has a great video about with whom you fly, within which he discusses eagles not flying with pigeons. Not everyone is equipped to soar to the heights you intend to reach. You can equip them if they are willing, but if they are not willing, leave them on the level they are comfortable with and have no guilt about doing so.

Tip

Do not allow dead weight to sink you. You can save someone from drowning, but not at the expense of risking your life. If it comes down to both of you drowning because they refuse to help themselves, then the choice is simple.

Quote

"Examine who you're trying to fly with and make sure they are not clipping your wings while you sleep."— "Kirk Alexander, Coach, Speaker, Trainer, Leadership developer, and Author."

THE LONG GAME

Life is too short to be investing time and money into something or someone that won't bring value to you or the team.

Scenario

Greg started a company where he would be providing leadership development and executive coaching services. He built it up over the course of two years and left his job to build his business full time. Greg was making a substantial income and realized he needed someone else to help him handle the workload. He asked his friend Brad to join him in the business. Since Brad had no coaching experience, he would need to go through certification. Greg was willing to cover 75 percent of the $6,000 fee for Brad's certification. Brad was not willing to invest the remaining $1,500. Greg asked their mutual friend Rachel, and she jumped at the opportunity. Brad asked Greg to meet for dinner. While at dinner, Brad expressed that he felt betrayed by Greg. Greg was furious and responded with, "How dare you ..."

Perspective

Cost versus value is a general concept that one seeks to strike the right balance between the cost of an action or item and its overall benefit. For example, if an item costs a certain amount yet has little overall value, that cost is not justified. If a person is remodeling their kitchen, they may consult a realtor to make sure they are not spending more than the return they will get for the investment. Similarly, you should take this approach when looking to add value to yourself. Is the cost worth the value?

You probably would not want to spend $40,000 to $50,000 on a doctorate that would only increase your salary by $2,000 a year, unless you just wanted to have the prestige and personal pride of having "Doctor" in front of your name. The Internet is full of courses that cost thousands of dollars and claim to increase your value in the workplace. Many of them do provide value and can increase your earning potential. However, you must examine the cost versus the value it will bring and determine if it is worth the cost. If it is worth the cost, then go for it. Always be willing to bet on yourself once you determine that the value is worth the cost. If you're offered the opportunity to level up and the value outweighs the cost, take the leap. Don't let the cost stop you from taking advantage of a life-changing situation. Say "Yes, I'm in," and figure out how to come up with the money later.

On the other hand, as an individual, you should ensure that you are bringing more value than it costs to have you around. That goes for the workplace and the circle of people that you associate with or conduct business with. If you are more trouble than the value you bring, do not be surprised if people are shedding you from their circle. You should also shed people from your circle who are too costly for the value they bring. That cost may come in the form of payroll, stress, drama, or the negativity they bring.

Tip

Focus on being a person who seeks to add value to others, and you will always be worth the cost. Invest in those who have the want and the will. Their return may not be seen right away, but remember … you are training your replacements.

Quote

"Price is what you pay monetarily, cost is what usually goes unseen; the grind, the late hours, and the sacrifices. Don't confuse price with cost. The value doesn't always equate."— "Gilda Alexander, exceptional wife, mother, and Command Chief Master Sargent United States Air Force."

PULL UP TO MOVE UP

Pull-ups are one of the toughest physical exercises for most people to do. It can be even more difficult to develop someone and pull them up to your level so that you can take the next step.

Scenario

Ann is a security specialist for a tech firm in Austin, Texas. The security manager she's worked under for two years has taken a position with a new startup company in Silicon Valley. Ann is excited about the opportunity to possibly step into what may be her dream job. During her final interview, she was told she would not be promoted. Ann asked what the reason was so that she could improve her chances next time. She was told it was easier to bring in a new security manager than to replace her position. She was doing a phenomenal job, and they could not imagine anyone else filling her role. Ann felt deflated and expressed that it was not her …

Perspective

In order to move up, you have to pull up. This means that you as a mentor have to pour into someone else who will replace you when you move up. If you are a valuable employee and excel at your position, your opportunity for advancement may be hindered by the fact that your superiors don't know how to effectively replace you, instead of you being scared to teach others the skills and knowledge to do your job for fear of losing it. Get to work on creating a suitable replacement to step into your current role so that you're available to move up, or get a job with a different organization that understands you can't keep good employees by keeping them down. Ideally they'll promote from within and keep the institutional knowledge , instead of losing that along with the employee. It goes back to the old African-American proverb of "each one teaches one." Do not hoard the skills and knowledge all to yourself. This applies whether you are moving up in an organization or moving on from one.

A great approach is to create a system for training your replacement. That can include a checklist of things you will do to prepare them, such as introducing new material or tasks, a manual to follow if applicable, teaching them the right way and not how you do things, demonstrating so they see first hand, introducing them to people they need to know or communicate with, and so on. Having a system in place allows you to replicate the process consistently and continue to pull a replacement up so you can move up. If you remain in the organization, provide mentorship and support to whomever you pull up. This approach is a phenomenal way to advance in any organization.

Tip

Always survey the talent around you and look for opportunities to mentor. See who is driven and looking to advance the right way.

Quote

"The greatest success we'll know is helping others succeed and grow."— "Gregory Scott Reid, bestselling author and world renowned keynote speaker."

YOU ARE NOT PRIME

Don't be afraid to surround yourself with intelligent people that will both challenge you and push you to new heights. You are not required to be the smartest person within your circle.

Scenario

John is the franchise owner of a home-inspection business. His company is doing well revenue-wise, but requires a lot of John's time. He has been looking to step back from the business to spend more time with his family. While interviewing candidates to hire, he comes across Frank, who is the former owner of a successful home inspection business that he sold for a nice nest egg. John realizes Frank has even more experience than he does, and feels a bit threatened by Frank's success in the home-inspection industry. After the interview, John gives it some careful consideration and decides ...

Perspective

When we think of prime, we usually think of a number greater than one that is not a product of two smaller numbers. Similarly, an individual could believe that they are prime and think that two other people together cannot equal what they do. It is even worse if they believe that they are the only person capable or the only person who should be responsible for particular tasks or operations within the organization. As the saying goes, "Everyone is replaceable." Stop feeling threatened by having other talented people around you.

The most accomplished and respected leaders usually have highly talented people around them. More specifically, they are surrounded by individuals who have talents that they do not have themselves. While interviewing an exceptional leader for the book, that leader said that, "It is easy to come up with a great idea on your own, but a game-changing idea takes place when talented people around you refine your idea further to have maximum effectiveness." Accepting that other people can improve upon a leader's idea can increase profits by eliminating costly oversights that can occur from that one individual making decisions on the entire process. Having talent around you will challenge you to become the best version of yourself. You can rely on this talent to perform responsibilities at a high level while you focus on the path forward. Todd Simmons, who is the owner of Courageous Leadership Alliance, has a phenomenal job title. His business card states that he is the chief vision officer of his company. When I first received his business card, I immediately envisioned him in his office late at night, plotting the path forward for the company and allowing his talented team to execute it. Build a phenomenal team and understand that you are not prime.

Tip

Surround yourself with talented people who challenge you to be the best version of yourself and allow you to do what you do best.

Quote

"It doesn't make sense to hire smart people and then tell them what to do; we hire smart people so they can tell us what to do."— "Steve Jobs, American entrepreneur and co-founder of Apple."

EMPEROR'S CLOTHES

Swallow your pride. Speak up

Scenario

Joseph, an up-and-coming mid-level manager, is one of the team leads for an aviation firm. Late hours and unexpected weekend overtime became a norm in the company. As far as all the team members knew, things were going well and the bottom line was getting better. The team did not understand why the schedule kept getting worse. Joseph decided to approach the manager to discuss morale and the operations tempo. To his surprise, the meeting he scheduled with the manager was canceled three times. Joseph, out of frustration, decided to go into the manager's office to see if he was in. As he walked in, he noticed that there were a group of senior executives and the managers enjoying a glass of wine and laughing. On the PowerPoint screen, he saw a glimpse of the proposal for next year's plan. It made him very uncomfortable to know that the company was pushing hard and reaping major rewards on the backs of the team members. There was never a why articulated, nor an end goal provided down the chain. There was no foreseeable end to the constant grind. Joseph felt moved to …

Perspective

Leaders are obligated to take care of those under their charge. Being honest is a virtue that must not be sacrificed. When a culture is created that lacks communication and accountability, there tends to be a climate of aggressive behaviors. Once this starts, individuals will choose to hold tightly to information and will not share it unless it becomes criminal or a danger to their livelihoods. Team members need to also understand that they have an obligation to tell the truth and not add fuel to the fire. If the baby is ugly, then call it ugly.

Pride is known to corrupt good people into bad situations. Many times, it's about re-ordering one's responsibilities and principles. Be honest with those around you. Take ownership of the things that you are part of. Never fail to do what is right and speak up. Bad news travels fast; good news wins hearts and minds. Leaders who focus on getting likes will lose momentum. Leaders who practice and execute leadership will earn the trust of those they lead.

Tip

Once a week, request a meeting with someone in the organization or in close proximity to a situation that you are working. Tell the individual how you handled the situation. Ask for feedback. Ensure the culture you are creating allows for open communication. Listen, learn, and level the playing field.

Quote

"Take care of your people, and they will take care of the mission. There are times when the mission will require more from your people. Never sacrifice people for the mission. People will work harder and smarter when led by credible and trustworthy leaders."— Natalie Castille

DON'T SH*T WHERE YOU EAT

Maintaining professional relationships in the workplace has a significant impact on the bottom line.

Scenario

Samuel sat through the annual corporate training and took copious notes. At the end of the day, he returned to his notes from the course hour that focused on unprofessional relationships. He recalls the instructor saying, "Personal relationships that cannot be managed professionally should be avoided or discouraged in the workplace. If you're the leader, set the standards and expectations for yourself and others. There are many cases where an office romance turns into a relationship that leads to a happy marriage. More often than not, however, it creates drama through tension, favoritism, and even hostility once the relationship sours." Samuel begins to play back a situation he sees brewing with two employees. He is now worried. He decides that on Monday he will …

Perspective

Let us examine the following situation that occurred when the relationship was not professional. Kyle was a manager for a life insurance company in Texas. An agent from another manager's team named Dwayne was going to be let go for lack of production. Kyle felt that Dwayne was not appropriately trained, and offered him a chance to join his team instead of being terminated. He discussed with him the standards and expectations, but did not emphasize any one rule more than the others. After training Dwayne and equipping him to earn good money, Dwayne began having an affair with Felicia, the top earner on Kyle's sales team. Both of these agents were married at the time they started seeing each other. Felicia's husband discovered the affair and forced her to quit working for the company. Kyle also fired Dwayne, so it was extremely costly to the company and his own bottom line due to the fact it was all commission-driven sales.

After that catastrophe, Kyle made very clear to all his new hires that inter-office relationships were frowned upon and discouraged. They all received the "Do not Sh*t Where You Eat" speech. It was a very expensive lesson for Kyle to learn. Today, most companies have policies that forbid relationships between supervisors and subordinates, peers, etc. in hopes of avoiding sexual-harassment litigation. If you do not set this expectation, be warned that there will be drama that could jeopardize the morale of your entire organization.

Tip

*"Do not sh*t where you eat."*

Quote

"Managing personal relationships at work can be like walking a greased tightrope with alligators below."— "Floyd Thomas, loving father, husband, and Retired Senior Master Sargent United States Air Force."

THAT'S NOT MY JOB

Time is money, and I do not get paid for this.

Scenario

Lisa has been working at a marketing firm for just less than four years. During her annual review, she asks her boss if she will be considered for a promotion. Her boss is taken back by the question because the position Lisa is asking about has more responsibility and requires doing whatever is needed to complete marketing campaigns. He replies, "I didn't think you would be interested in that position because whenever I ask you to do anything extra or pick up the slack for a team member, you say that it's not your job." Lisa realizes her words and actions have come back to bite her. Her lack of commitment to the company's vision and the related goals that contributed to the team's success were not her focus. Her only response is …

Perspective

When I hear the phrase "That is not my job," in the workplace, several thoughts come to mind. From the perspective of an employee, it could mean several things. The employee may be selfish and only concerned with tasks that benefit them or are required of them. They may not feel like a valued member of the team or part of the team at all. If not corrected, this attitude will lead to workplace issues among your staff.

From the standpoint of the leader, it usually means the vision has not been clearly articulated and goals have not been established. If an employee has not bought into the vision or has not had it explained clearly to them, the potential for buy-in is slim to none. The leader has to ensure the vision of the organization is clearly disseminated directly to the employees. Once there is belief in the vision, it sparks a team mentality that transitions from "That is not my job," to "What do you need me to do?" When your team has this kind of ladder mentality, the goals and subsequent tasks will be accomplished both efficiently and effectively.

Tip

As the leader, it is essential to identify key players and stakeholders in your organization who have complete buy-in and can help motivate others to buy into the vision themselves. Cast the vision and explore how others feel. Gather concerns. Adjust if needed.

Quote

"A vision is not just a picture of what could be; it is an appeal to our better selves, a call to become something more."— "Rosabeth Moss Kanter, professor of business at Harvard Business School."

YOU ARE THE PROBLEM

It is not you, it is me. Maybe you heard this from an ex-partner who is severing ties with you. Possibly you are discussing your frustration with a process and cannot articulate the true essence of your feelings. What if you are the common denominator with the things that happen negatively in your life ...

Scenario

Kris is two years from retirement. To many in the organization, he has already tapped out. Kris lacks drive and motivation. There are currently four major projects that Kris is a team member of. He hasn't successfully produced any of the products that he is the lead on. On multiple occasions, when asked where his deliverables were, he gave an excuse and blamed others for his failures. Kris thought of himself highly and had a belief that others around him were incompetent and the reason for the problems. However, he never saw where his own actions were detrimental to the team. When Kris walked into work today, he was given a bit of humble pie. The leader of his division had requested to see him and was standing by to inform him that ...

Perspective

One tends to look at their surroundings and assess what he or she controls. The things that are not in our control we tend to place in a bin labeled *I do not own, so therefore not my fault.* Whether you are a leader or a follower, you have ownership of everything that touches your space. You may not be the decision-maker or the executor in some instances, but if it affects you or your team in any way, own it. When we do not own or take responsibility for things within the areas that we spend time in, we go into blaming and projecting the burden onto others. Through the years, we have learned that individuals collecting a paycheck are doing just that: Collecting a paycheck. I am not inferring the work one accomplishes does not deserve compensation. We are saying that there is more to working than just showing up. What is an intrinsic value to you can lead to an extrinsic value for others. If or when problems do come your way, the problems are accepted, and efforts to mitigate them are at the forefront.

Tip

Take inventory of the last five problems you had to solve. Create a square chart. Place each of the stakeholders in their respective squares. Notice where you are on this chart. Are there problems that you created? Were there problems you solved? How many levels of approval did it go through from where you sat? How do you increase your problem-solving matrix position or ability to influence the decisions?

Quote

"One cannot resolve an issue if one is stuck on the issue or the problem. To become mired in a problem where there is no possibility of a resolution means that there is no will to move beyond the problem."— "Catherine Pulsifer, author of Change Your Life."

YOUR ROUTINE SUCKS

Are your daily routines contributing to or derailing your growth and success?

Scenario

Peter had his sights set on making his college's golf team. He has sacrificed spending time with his buddies to put in work at the driving range and on the course. Every time they try to get him to join them for a fun night out, he declines by saying he must stick to his routine. When he is at the range, he motivates himself by saying, "Practice makes perfect." Tryouts arrive, and Peter does not make the cut. He is extremely frustrated and stops by the coach's office for feedback. The coach highlights some things he needs to work on. Peter tells the coach about the number of hours he has been practicing. Coach tells him that it's not how much you practice but practicing the right way. He tells Peter that "Perfect practice makes perfect, not practice makes perfect." Peter was distraught but knew he needed to …

Perspective

Establishing a routine is critical to achieving your dreams or being successful in your career. However, if your routines are built on a foundation of bad habits, then success will be hard to come by. That's why it is important to establish a routine that is designed to achieve a particular goal or lifestyle. This is true for both personal and career success.

I've worked with plenty of individuals who tell me about waking up at 3 a.m. to start their day. When I inquire about what that looks like, it is usually drinking coffee and watching TV. Waking up at 3 a.m. is useless unless there is a purpose behind it. You have to implement positive daily habits that will contribute to your success. We usually get stuck in a pattern that prevents us from doing what we need to do. We become aware and usually blame or attack ourselves. Instead, focus on changing the behavior pattern that is hindering us from achieving our goals. Research the routines of people who have the level of success you are working to achieve. You may experience more success by tackling one area at a time, slowly replacing negative patterns with positive ones.

Tip

Starting with small incremental changes will be easier to maintain. Drastically changing your entire life is difficult for anyone to maintain.

Quote

"Depending on what they are, our habits will either make us or break us. We become what we repeatedly do."— "Sean Covey, American Author."

RUN WITH 'EM

We all have scars. We get to choose whether we run from them or run with them.

Scenario

On a beautiful summer day in August, Jessica and her entire family met in the park to celebrate her grandparents' diamond wedding anniversary. Everyone was catching up and enjoying the festivities. Chad, a cousin of Jessica's whom she hadn't seen in years, ran up from behind to give her a bear hug. Jessica responded with a right elbow to Chad's temple, followed by a kick to the groin area. Chad had no idea Jessica was the victim of an attempted sexual assault while away at college. She had since taken self-defense classes so she would be better prepared to fight off an attacker. The family was in complete shock by her violent reaction to the hug. Jessica looked down at Chad and screamed …

Perspective

Over the last few years, I have devoted a lot of time to researching resiliency, leadership, and self-awareness. The vast majority of it—99.9 percent—was for my own personal growth during personal times of hardship. My focus has since shifted to helping others, but before that could happen, I had to heal first. The realization is that we encounter the world through our own lens, and once we hit a wall and get through it, we are able to share this lens with others. Both unfortunately and fortunately, the scars remain after you've healed as a reminder that you are still here pushing! Not all scars are visible. Some may be emotional, physical, or spiritual. Seek help in healing. Seek that one person who listens more than speaks. Heal correctly and within your own time. The road may be difficult, but own it without shame and without judgment. Your difficult journey may be the light that someone else needs to keep moving forward toward healing and redemption.

Tip

We all have scars. Heal! Run in front of 'em. The road is filled with good human beings ready to run with you! It may be a sprint for some, a marathon for others. Just start the journey. We will help you finish!

Quote

"It has been said, 'time heals all wounds.' I do not agree. The wounds remain. In time, the mind, protecting its sanity, covers them with scar tissue and the pain lessens. But it is never gone."—"Rose Fitzgerald Kennedy, American philanthropist."

TUNNEL EFFECT

What or who is your why? What is driving your motivation?

Scenario

Dave has been building a landscaping empire since graduating from high school. Without a college degree, he is earning a six-figure income. Dave is married with two young kids. His wife has been there from the beginning, watching Dave work seven days a week consistently for the last four years. She has tried to convince Dave to hire a manager and spend more time with her and the kids. Dave has been looking forward to his class reunion to impress his classmates with his success in achieving the American dream. Two weeks before the reunion, while at work, a gentleman asks someone on Dave's crew where they can find him. Dave overhears the gentleman and approaches him. The gentleman hands Dave an envelope and says, "You've been served." After opening the envelope, he rushes home, only to find …

Perspective

The grind does not stop! Many of our teammates spend countless hours on the job. Timelines open and close. New tasks take our attention from old tasks. We clock out of work and try to experience life to the best of our abilities. Personal obligations are now in focus. Other commitments shape the afternoon until the late evening. In the blink of an eye, it is time for bed and dreams are upon us.

For many, that is the scenario. A new day brings new opportunities. For others, we have become complacent. Instead of separating our lives from what we have to do versus what we need to do, one part of our lives consumes us. Work becomes constant, without shutting off our brains. Instead of drawing a line in the sand, it becomes a seamless adventure to knock tasks out and accomplish goals. Maybe your sights are on a promotion or some other lofty goal. What are you sacrificing? Your team? Commitments? Family? Your faith? The tunnel does not stop unless something that you have no control over creates a barrier. Once you hit that wall, it is hard to recover.

Tip

Prioritize the things in your life and assign value. What has your daily focus? What are you unable to shut off when you clock out? Create a line in the sand, and ensure there is a line of demarcation separating your time and the things you value.

Quote

"We are what we repeatedly do. Excellence, then, is not an act but a habit."— "Will Durant, American writer."

YOUR MOMMA DON'T WORK HERE

Don't depend on others to clean up after you or to have your best interests in mind. Take pride in your work and take the initiative.

Scenario

Rosa is a Master Sergeant in the Air Force who has become frustrated with the evaluations submitted to her by the supervisors. She spends time at home reviewing them and making countless corrections, which takes time away from her family. This is a recurring problem every time they submit evaluations or promotion packages for the Airmen they supervise. They quickly submit subpar evaluations and packages, knowing that Rosa will make them look spectacular. In the beginning, they submitted packages that they spent days working on, only to have Rosa mark up countless corrections. She then decided it was easier and faster to make the corrections herself rather than have the supervisors correct them. Rosa now regrets making that decision. She decided to have a meeting with them after reaching her breaking point. As soon as they are seated in the conference room, she pushes the most recently submitted evaluations in front of them and says ...

Perspective

This particular area of truth is not about your messy coworkers. It's about cleaning up someone else's work instead of teaching them the proper way. Too often, when someone has turned in subpar work, we take the easy way out by saying, "It will be faster if I do it myself." This mentality can cripple your workforce by not showing them how to get it done right and to the expected standard. Even if it means something may be late, take the time to have the employee finish their work, with your guidance, to the standards you expect. Then they will not only know what is expected, but to what standard and you can then hold them accountable.

I had two employees in the office who were turning in subpar work, and often right up to the deadline. I instituted a policy to have them send their work to each other and copy me on it. They were to edit each other's work and send it back. The first time editing, they destroyed each other's work with corrections and were ashamed that I could see all the corrections since the document was shared among the three of us. After about the third time, neither document needed correcting since they were going through their own work with a fine-tooth comb so someone else would not have to correct it. I sat with them and explained how impressed I was with the quality of work they were submitting to me. If I had taken the easy way out, thinking I could just correct it myself faster, it would have saved time initially, but would have left me constantly correcting both of their work and taking my time away from more important tasks.

Tip

Taking the time to show someone the right way to do something and setting the expectation is always worth it.

Quote

"The best kind of accountability on a team is peer-to-peer. Peer pressure is more efficient and effective than going to the leader, anonymously complaining, and having them stop what they are doing to intervene."— "Patrick Lencioni, American author."

BOY BYE

Check yourself before you wreck yourself, and others. Means to go ahead with yourself... Get out of someone's face...-Urban Dictionary

Scenario

Over the past few days, I have been surrounded by amazing women and men from around the world. It was truly amazing. I was called by my rank and official title so many times. My assumption is that this title and rank have bestowed upon me great responsibilities and the trust of many above me to work for those I am charged with leading. It is a great feeling to have that much power. Of course, some things are beneath me … Whoaaaah …

Perspective

I get home from the work conference, and I am immediately reminded that my rank stops at the doorway to our home. I announce to my wife that the chief is home, to which she responds, "Boy Bye." Ego is no place for a home or your workplace. Continue to strengthen your strengths and improve on your weaknesses. Humility is intrinsic, but arrogance is felt by others. Rank or job title does not follow you home. Continue to be a student of your craft and always do the work that got you there!!! If you forget, there is always one person who can and will set you back on track! Get to work!

Tip

Reminder: Stay humble!

Quote

"Humility is royalty without a crown."— "Spencer W. Kimball, American religious leader."

THERE IS ALWAYS SOMEONE BETTER

You are not that good … thought I should break the ice with that statement. One day you will come to the realization that someone is working harder than you are. Your routine sucks, your energy is off, and somehow you blame others. Well, get over yourself. Pick your head up and grind.

Scenario

We're always trying to keep our son active, so we enrolled him in jujitsu for the summer. After his first week of training, they were paired up to spar against one another. He was able to handle the kid he was up against fairly easily and tap him out a couple of times. He was so excited to give my wife a play-by-play of his takedowns. After my son went upstairs to shower, my wife said I should talk to him so he could be more humble. I told her there was no need and that he would be humbled in due time. The next week he was paired up with a different partner that was smaller but more skilled. Every time my son tried to attack, he was taken down to the mat and forced into submission. When we returned home, my wife asked how the class was, and he responded with ok, then began to head upstairs. I told him to come back downstairs and give mama the play-by-play like last week. He looked at her and said sadly …

Perspective

Self-doubt creeps in, and then your motivation sinks. It will be hard for you to get out of the rut that comes along with a negative mindset. We compare ourselves to those around us and wonder what extra they have that allowed them to achieve that level of success. Working in an organization, I would frequently see colleagues taking a tally of who has something that they did not. It can be an award, a better car, or maybe a better position. We then place more value on what we do while not considering the grind or grit it took for them to get there. It is time to look at yourself in the mirror and do some self-reflection and goal setting. The time is now. Spend more time comparing your current self to your former self rather than comparing yourself to others around you. If you have achieved a high level of success, it is okay to enjoy it and be proud of yourself. Never stop putting the work in unless you're prepared to step aside.

Tip

Take inventory of your life. Develop a system to help organize your life. Plan your steps. Be open to change. There are multiple roads to the center of a town. If not, create one.

Quote

"There is always someone better than you. Whatever it is that you do for a living, chances are you will run into a situation in which you are not as talented as the person next to you. That's when being a competitor can make a difference in your fortunes."— "Pat Summitt, served as the head coach of the University of Tennessee Lady Vols basketball team from 1974-2012."

FEELS LOW/HIGH

Take a ruler out and measure your arms. Afterward, measure the distance you want to go in life. Is it two paces forward, or 100 miles beyond what your eyes can see? Now that you have both distances, measure the distance from your head to your heart. What are you willing to put your mind and heart through to reach where you want to go?

Scenario

Kendall, a level headed HR manager, was reflecting on his past four years with the company. He was amazed by how he and the team accomplished so much in a short amount of time. As much as Kendall had a lot to celebrate, he became a bit down thinking about his personal goals. He failed to accomplish any of the five personal goals he had written. Kendall has a passion for creating and designing homes. As a young adult, he won many awards and accolades that proved to many that he was likely to achieve greatness in that industry. However, Kendall decided to join an organization that ensured he had a salary and healthcare benefits. He got comfortable. He realized that this company had grown tremendously through his hard work. However, his pay, benefits, and progression upward have not changed. Kendall does not want to sacrifice what he has now to pursue his dreams. Instead, Kendall decided to speak to his life coach about where he was in life. He started the conversation by saying ...

Perspective

An old supervisor frequently told me to figure it out. I would get frustrated because he knew all the answers, but wanted me to do the work to find the answer I was looking for. In my head, it seemed logical that if he gave me the answer, it would be more efficient than me looking for it on my own. My supervisor taught me the power of a strong work ethic and the ability to go and seek. There were times I pretended to go and find the answer. Other times I took a shortcut. I realized eventually that failing to go and discover the answers did not hurt my supervisor, it hurt me. My development took a long route. When things seem out of reach, bring them into focus. When tasks seem too easy, did you misjudge them? How real are your expectations? Do you search with your eyes open or closed?

Tip

Simply do the work and stay the course. Short cuts lead to long lessons. Take out a blank sheet of paper and draw a circle. Place a dot in the middle of the circle. Place the pencil down. That dot is you. Figure out a way to expand your circle of knowledge. What is needed in your circle to enable you to grow? Write five things that will increase the strength of your circle.

Quote

In the measurement world, we set a goal and strive to achieve it. In the universe of possibility, we set the context and let life unfold.— "Benjamin Zander, English conductor."

HORSE'S MOUTH

What is your information source? How frequently do you connect to this source? Do you trust this source?

Scenario

Lowell is the gossip in the unit. He always gets the best knowledge about people, situations, and perceptions of those close to the event. It seems that Lowell is always front and center in the information space. What makes it astonishing is that people bring the information to him without his solicitation. It has become his trademark and part of his character. Problems began when Lowell began to repeat the information he was hearing. Since he was perceived as credible, others ran with the information and told others the news they had received from Lowell. As Lowell entered the front door of the organization, security asked him to stop and walk with them to the deputy director's office. Lowell had an assumption of what he was being called in to discuss. As he sat in the chair, the deputy director walked in. Lowell immediately began apologizing for …

Perspective

Grandparents are a wealth of knowledge. Many would quote an old folk tale or a parable from a popular book. When I would share a story with my grandmother, she would ask, "Did you hear it from the horse's mouth or the horse's backside? I did not understand that saying until my teenage years. What she was articulating was the need for my information to be correct.

Do not pass information to others that did not come from a credible source. Information that comes from one person about another person needs to be checked. Furthermore, not all news is yours to carry. Focus on the information that is in your need-to-know territory. Everything else is gossip.

Tip

Write down or take a mental inventory of the information that is shared with you. Do not change words and do not add them. Read what you wrote three times. Now ask yourself, how does this information add value to my professional life or personal life? Does it help others succeed? Do I need this information? If so, act. If not, discard. This practice will help you eliminate unwanted noise.

Quote

"Gossip is just a tool to distract people who have nothing better to do from feeling jealous of those few of us still remaining with noble hearts."— "Anna Godbersen, American writer."

YOU DON'T OWN THE RIGHTS

Have you ever worked hard on a project only to have someone take it to the finish line? Have you ever worked hard on a project and others received all the credit? Have you ever put so much energy into a piece of art (work), and no recognition or acknowledgment was given? If yes, thanks for doing your job ... you got paid!

Scenario

John was an employee for a company that manages housing on military installations. Every time a family moved out, he conducted an inspection and determined what charges needed to be assessed for damages. John and other agents made calculations to determine how much the family owed for items like carpet, based on when it was installed and the date they moved out. John had a previous job as an IT developer, so he created software to make the calculations automatic by simply entering the dates. John received an offer from a competing housing contractor and accepted. After putting in his two-week notice, he was informed that the software belonged to his employer since it was developed while they were paying him. John was upset and threatened to ...

Perspective

For many, the above questions and final statement probably will lead to some scarred tissue or feelings of neglect. Please put this in perspective. In the job you are in, I would bet that you are getting paid. There is a benefits package attached to it. Additionally, there may be a severance package, if warranted. One of my close friends worked for a prominent place of business that required him to lead teams to think up some pretty amazing things. His team would create, design, build, and deliver more frequently than not. Besides a pat on the back and a cursory thank you, there were not any grand parades or formal recognition boards. He felt slighted and not valued. One day a respected leader told him, "You don't own those ideas while you are on the clock." For some jobs, you are on the clock all day, every day. Do not stop giving to the organization that pays you to think. However, do not be so tied to a project that you are unable to release it both mentally and emotionally.

Tip

Check your passion and emotions. It is okay to have passion for something that you are working on. If emotions lead your conversation on the topic, it may prevent you from being truly unbiased and too attached to the result. When one becomes emotional during a process, he or she may not be able to contain the real emotions that accompany it, therefore they may appear to have a lack of emotional intelligence. Take time to understand your passion for your work and the emotions that accompany it. Realize how it makes you feel and ensure it does not get in the way of preventing its success.

Quote

"Incredible change happens in your life when you decide to take control of what you do have power over instead of craving control over what you don't."—"Steve Maraboli, philanthropist."

#FACTS

What they said!

Scenario

Brandon and Kala are now in their fifth year of marriage. Their social media presence shows a glamorous life of love and admiration for each other. In reality, all is not what it seems. Brandon does not like feedback, nor does he like receiving criticism from anyone close to him. It is not that he lacks respect for his closest friends; he is comfortable with rebutting the information, which leads to an argument every time. In an effort not to cause any friction, Kala only responds with statements that Brandon wants to hear.

Brandon has a big event coming up and, as always, asks his wife how he looks in his fancy new suit. In her haste, Kala failed to look completely at the whole outfit. For the parts she saw, she thought it was okay. The suit was a little small, but if she had given that feedback, it would have led to an all-out confrontation about his weight and eating habits. Brandon and Kala had a great time at the event. Brandon felt that it was a success. When he opened up his social media, he found hundreds of pictures of him posted with nasty comments and rude statements. Brandon looked at Kala and asked if she felt that some of the statements on social media were true. Kala decided that enough was enough. Kala said ...

Perspective

What you need to hear is not always what you want to hear. To know and not do is worse than doing things accidentally. Many times, we hear hashtag facts after someone says something that connects. A hashtag is placed because it now connects to all of the other times someone has correlated that same theme. What do you do with that information?

Facts are known to be true. As leaders, we take facts and then we use them to make informed decisions. This is not about where we get information; this is about what we do with the information we receive. As leaders, facts are what keep us out of the red. As entrepreneurs, facts are what keep us in the green. Fact finders always have a leg up, because they are taking the time to filter the real from the erroneous. They filter the information and place it into bins that allow for easy reading and articulation of key points. Fact finders understand that time is of the essence, and the requirement to be correct is their default. Check your understanding and articulate what you know.

Tip

Fact-check the information you receive. If you have some hesitation about the information, so will others. Repeat what you hear in your head and listen to the words. Does it pass the common sense test? How does it sound out in the open?

Quote

"You can spend your whole life building a wall of facts between you and anything real."— "Chuck Palahniuk, American journalist."

MOMENTS OF CLARITY

Kirk and Keith decided to write this book based on reflections from the heart. The planning of the book was easy. Creating the skeleton of the book was a fairly simple task. Writing the book was hard. Life does not stop. Over the years, we encountered multiple personal and professional situations that made us rethink the future of this book. Each and every page was hand-curated and heart-inspired. Not a day went by that we did not think about the sacrifices of our mentors, who poured into us constantly. We reflect on our kids, family members, and, most importantly, our significant others, Gilda and Natalie, who motivated us throughout the process.

MENTORS

Mentors are crucial to our success. They help us achieve our goals more expediently. Mentors can also reduce or eliminate some pain points by sharing their mistakes from their own journey. Seek out a mentor who is successful in the area you are seeking to excel in. Do not be afraid to reach out to mentors who have failed and persevered. There were many mentors who inspired this collaborative effort, and we will surely miss some. We thank any and all mentors who gave us the inspiration to lead, learn, and fight to be in the room. We not only have a seat at the table, we are building our own table for new leaders to have a seat at!!!

FAMILY

To Natalie: My number one fan, my world, my everything. I thank you for being the human being I needed in my life. I remember when we first committed ourselves to each other. Our commitment was never to fix each other, but to be the best versions of who we want to be and to love and learn together. We vowed never to change each other. We lied! You have been my guiding light, my counselor, and the glue that keeps my world intact. I thank you for helping me find the man I needed to be. I thank you for pushing me to greatness and never allowing me to be less than what I am capable of being. You do not just support my dreams; you help create them. Thank you for loving me conditionally. Yes, conditionally. Your words were, "How can I love you if you do not love yourself?" Thank you for teaching me how to love me again so I can love you from the depths of my soul. Lastly, thank you for believing in me. Without you, my dreams would only be dreams. God guided us to each other. God brought us together. All Glory to God!

From: Your loving husband, Keith

To Gilda: You are my best friend and the most amazing wife a man could be blessed to have. Throughout your decorated military career, I have been the soil to your flower, nurturing and supporting so you can accomplish your goals and be the best you can be. You are such an amazing example to our kids of what it is to be a mom boss. You are and will continue to be the glue that holds our family close. I look forward to the next chapter where you enjoy your retirement and transition to being the soil to my flower. Although, being the dedicated, driven, and passionate person that you are, I'm not sure when that will be. Your continued support is what allows me to always have the confidence to take the leap and do what brings me joy and purpose. Thank you for all that you do. I love you more than you'll ever know.

From: Your loving husband, Kirk

OUR OBLIGATION

Our obligation in writing this book was to be authentic and open. People are most inspired by individuals they share commonalities with. We desired to share our experiences, both good and bad, in a way that could be used as a learning tool to inspire thought and conversation. We were both raised in Lafayette, Louisiana, but have traveled abroad and been exposed to cultures and people that have helped shape us into who we are and how we think, and have inspired us in various ways. Remaining authentic to who we are allows us to navigate environments across the spectrum, such as the streets of the neighborhood, the classroom, boardroom, military, and so on. We also feel an obligation to share our knowledge and experiences with as many people as possible to assist them in their journeys to success. Our obligation is also to ourselves, to hold each other accountable to be exceptional husbands, fathers, mentors, and men of character who are role models for the next generation.

WHAT'S NEXT

As the world continues to evolve and present new challenges, we will adapt, learn, and develop new leadership focus areas to guide the current and next generation of leaders. Our approach will always be agile, yet able to connect to all audiences on a deeper level. On our social media platforms, we will share knowledge, inspire leaders, and deliver actionable steps to accelerate change. We look forward to the opportunity to learn with and from all those we encounter on the journey to success through personal and leadership development.

AUTHOR INSIGHTS

Kirk's Insight

My journey to becoming an author has been inspired in various ways. From growing up in Lafayette, Louisiana, to serving in the Air Force, to my work as an educator, to fatherhood, and to serving as a military spouse to my inspirational wife. Eight years ago, I decided to become an educator in hopes of inspiring future generations. I enjoyed working with students daily to consistently improve and reach new heights. However, I quickly found myself wanting to spend more time teaching them leadership and life skills than traditional school subjects. I've always been one to pass on to others the knowledge and skills I've learned. Inspired by a conversation with my childhood best friend, I decided to take the leap and become a coach, speaker, and trainer. Having the opportunity to work with leaders of companies and the U.S. military is an honor. My mission is to develop dynamic leaders who accelerate change and positively affect culture. Since there are a limited number of people who can be reached through training or speaking engagements, I wanted to become an author to share what I've learned and continue to learn with anyone seeking self-improvement. This book is the first of a series to inspire and develop the next generation of leaders.

Keith's Insight

Every good story starts with "There I was …" Well, mines starts with where I was not! While looking for fulfillment and an identity, I decided to enlist into the United States Air Force. Having served more than twenty-seven years, there is no way looking back would ever be an option. Mentors and trusted partners guided me through trials and tribulations, allowing me to self-examine and grow into the human being I desired to be. People are my passion, and serving this great nation is something I cherish every day. It's said there comes a moment in your life when you become invested in the things you love and your path becomes clear. Since discovering my path, I have been charging forward with shaping lives and investing in others. Of all the accolades I have achieved throughout my career, what I am most proud of is being known for giving my all to develop others to be the best versions of themselves. I am a reflection of the village that raised me and continues to lift me with prayer. Who would have ever thought that an eighteen year old who left Lafayette, Louisiana, in 1995 would travel the world, reaching hundreds of thousands through inspirational instruction? God Did! As a certified International Speaker, Trainer, and Executive Coach, my goal is to add value wherever it is needed. I give God all the glory! Can't stop--will not stop!

Disclaimer: The views represented are those of the speaker or author and do not necessarily represent the views of DoD or its components.